DEMOS

Demos is an independent think tank committed to radical thinking on the long-term problems facing the UK and other advanced industrial societies.

It aims to develop the ideas - both theoretical and practical - that will help to shape the politics of the 21st century, and to improve the breadth and quality of political debate.

Demos publishes books and a quarterly journal and undertakes substantial empirical and policy-oriented research projects. It also runs a permanent computer conference.

In all its work **Demos** brings together people from a wide range of backgrounds in business, academia, government, the voluntary sector and the media to share and cross-fertilise ideas and experiences.

For further information please write to:

Demos
9 Bridewell Place
London EC4V 6AP

tel: 071 353 4479
fax: 071 353 4481
email: demos.demon.co.uk

JUBILEE CENTRE PUBLICATIONS LTD.

Alone Again:
Ethics After Certainty

Zygmunt Bauman

DEMOS

First published in 1994
by
Demos
9 Bridewell Place
London EC4V 6AP
tel: 071 353 4479
fax: 071 353 4481

© Demos 1994

All rights reserved

Paper No. 9

ISBN 1 898309 40 X

Cover illustration by Andrzej Krause

Printed in Great Britain by
White Dove Press
London
Typesetting by Bartle & Wade Associates

Contents

Foreword i

Introduction 1

The Rise of Reason: Bureaucracy and Business 3

Fragmentation and Discontinuity 15

The Privatisation of Common Fates 22

The Deficiencies of Community 30

Risk and Limits 34

New Ethics in Search of New Politics 39

Further Reading 46

Foreword

Throughout Demos' work, a continuing theme has been that as old ideologies wane, ethics necessarily become more important. But whereas in the past we could rest our ethics on solid foundations - such as the Church, tradition or faith in a utopia - today ethics have become far less certain and far more complex.

Zygmunt Bauman has now written for us a compelling account both of why the old arguments won't do and of how we should think about the new ethical landscape in which we live. Part of his argument concerns the changing nature of modern life: the spread of instrumental organisations, and the fragmentary and episodic character of the times. Its most notable feature, he argues, is that life has become privatised in far-reaching ways. For him privatisation is not primarily about the sale of old state industries. Instead he means a much more sweeping shift in the character of everyday lives and concerns that has made people more concerned with their own space and less willing to make commitments. Privatisation has brought many liberations. But it has eroded our capacity to think in terms of common interests and fates, contributing to the decay of an active culture of political argument and action.

Unfortunately, most of the conventional responses to this situation do not stand up to scrutiny. One is the sometimes sophisticated, sometimes naive, attempt to resurrect the community as a foundation for certainty and morality. As Bauman points out, the escape from the constraints and impositions of community has been the dominant story of the last 200 years: reversing it is more likely to put morality into a deep freeze than to resuscitate it. Much the same is true of the attempt to make the family a home for pure morality in an unfriendly world. Meanwhile the neutralisation of morality by business and bureaucracy, with their emphasis on rules rather than judgement, necessarily makes them unlikely candidates for any rebirth of ethics. Instead ours is an era in which morality rests with the individual, alone again with his or her choices, and no longer able to depend on old certainties. Whether we like it or not there are no longer any convincing external props or anchors.

Bauman's argument suggests that rather than returning to old beliefs we need to transcend the antimonies of traditional thought: of state versus market, individual versus community, which have so distorted much of our political culture. Only then can we better understand the connection, rather than contradiction, between the health of common institutions concerned for common fates and the active engagement of millions of questioning, self-directed and often awkward individuals.

Zygmunt Bauman is one of the world's foremost philosophers, who has written brilliantly on themes ranging from the Holocaust to mortality, post-modernity to politics. He does not offer a simple blueprint. Rather he offers a starting point for talking sense about an ethics fit for our times.

Geoff Mulgan

Our time thinks in terms of 'knowing how to do it', even where there is nothing to be done.

Karl Jaspers

We can now do what we want, and the only question is what do we want? At the end of our progress we stand where Adam and Eve once stood: all we are faced with now is the moral question.

Max Frisch

Introduction

The great Danish theologian and moral philosopher, Knud Logstrup, mused: 'It is a characteristic of human life that we mutually trust each other... Only because of some special circumstance do we ever distrust a stranger in advance... Initially we believe one another's word; initially we trust one another'.

Not so another religious philosopher, Leon Shestov, a Russian refugee and professor at the Sorbonne: *'Homo homini lupus* is one of the most steadfast maxims of eternal morality. In each of our neighbours we fear a wolf... We are so poor, so weak, so easily ruined and destroyed! How can we help being afraid!... We see danger, danger only...'

Surely, Logstrup and Shestov cannot both be right. Or can they? True, they contradict each other, but don't we all get contradictory signals from the experience of our own lives? Sometimes we trust, sometimes we fear. More often than not, we are not sure whether to trust and disarm, or to sniff danger and be on guard - and then we are confused and unsure what to do. Of which has there been more in our lives, of trust or of fear? The answer seems to depend on the kind of life we have lived.

Logstrup was born and died in tranquil, serene, peaceful Copenhagen, where the royals bicycled the streets together with their subjects. When they finished their rides they were able to leave their bicycles on the pavement knowing that, in the

1

absence of thieves, they would be there when they needed them again. Shestov was hunted down and refused university posts by the tsarist regime for being born in the wrong faith, then hunted down and exiled by the anti-tsarist revolution for professing the wrong faith, then drank his fill from the bitter chalice of exile in a foreign country. The two wise men reported two stridently different experiences. Their generalizations contradicted each other, but so did the lives they generalized from.

And this seems to apply to all of us. We generalize from what we see. Whenever we say 'people are what they are', what we mean is the people we meet; people shaped and moved and guided by the world we together happen to inhabit. And if we say once that people can be trusted, and at another time that they are wolves to be feared, and if both statements ring true or at least partly true - then it seems that what people are or appear to be depends, wholly or in part, on the kind of world we live in. Moreover, if what we think about each other reflects what we are, it is also true that what we are is itself a reflection of what we believe ourselves to be; the image we hold of each other and of all of us together has the uncanny ability to self-corroborate. People treated like wolves tend to become wolf-like; people treated with trust tend to become trust-worthy. What we think of each other matters.

We will never know for sure whether 'people as such' are good or evil (though perhaps we will go on and on quarrelling about it). But it does matter whether we believe them to be 'basically' good or evil, *moral* or *immoral*, and consequently how we treat them. What matters even more is whether people are trusted with the *capacity of making moral judgments*, and consequently considered to be *moral subjects* - that is, persons capable of bearing a *moral responsibility*, not just a legal one, for their deeds.

The Rise of Reason: Bureaucracy and Business

In 1651, at the dawn of what later came to be known as the modern era, Thomas Hobbes passed the verdict which was to guide the thought and action of modern legislators, educators and moral preachers:

...men have no pleasure (but on the contrary a great deale of griefe) in keeping company, where there is no power to overawe them all... And upon all signes of contempt, or undervaluing, naturally endeavours, as far as he dares (which amongst them that have no common power to keep them in quiet, is far enough to make them destroy each other,) to extort a greater value from its contemners, by dommage...

Hereby it is manifest, that during the time men live without a common Power to keep them all in awe, they are in that condition which we called Warre: and such a warre, as if of every man, against every man...

The message was straightforward: if you wish men to be moral, you must force them to be so. Only under the threat of pain will men stop paining each other. To stop fearing each other, men must fear a power superior to them all.

The corollary was another briefing: you cannot build on people's impulses, inclinations and predispositions. Their passions (that is, all passions except the passion for better life, the one passion that lends itself to logic and reason) must instead be rooted out or stifled. Instead of following their *feelings*, people should be taught, and forced if need be - to *calculate*. In a moral world, only the voice of reason should be heard. And a world in which only the voice of reason is heard is a moral world.

Thus arose the great divide which was to become the trademark of modern living: one between reason and emotion, taken to be the substance and the foundation of all life-and-death choices: like those between order and chaos, civilised life and the war of all against all. In particular, the divide separated the regular, predictable and controllable from the contingent, erratic, unpredictable and going out of hand. Indeed, for every problem there is by definition one, and only one, true, reason-dictated solution, but a virtually infinite variety of erroneous ones; where reason does not rule, 'everything may happen', and thus the whole situation is hopelessly beyond control.

The moral world can only be, therefore, a *regular, orderly* world (an 'orderly' world is one in which probabilities of events are not random; some events are considerably more probable than others, some have virtually no chance of happening). Moral persons cannot be buffeted by erratic impulses; they can only be guided, consistently and in a systematic fashion by laws, rules and norms; principles which clearly specify what in a given situation one should do and what one should desist from. Morality, like the rest of social life, must be founded on *Law*, and there must be an *ethical code* behind morality, consisting of prescriptions and prohibitions. Teaching or coercing people to be moral means making them obey that ethical code. By this reasoning, becoming moral' is equivalent to learning, memorising and following the *rules*.

Modernity came up with two great institutions meant to achieve that purpose; to assure the prevalence of morality through following rules. One was bureaucracy, the other was business. The two institutions differ from each other in many respects, and are often at loggerheads with each other, but they agree on one quite seminal thing: they are both bent on the eradication of emotions or at least keeping them off limit. Since they are enemies of affection, they have both been hailed since their inception as incarnations of rationality and instruments of rationalization. Each embarked on achieving the same effect in its own fashion.

Bureaucracy has been described by its theorists, beginning with the great German sociologist Max Weber, as the typically modern (and advanced) way of doing things. When a complex task needs the division of skills and labour of many people, each doing but a part of the task and not necessarily aware of what the whole task consists of, all efforts must be dovetailed and coordinated so that the overall objective may be reached.

The specifically bureaucratic way of running things is founded on a strict chain of command and equally strict definitions of the roles ascribed to every link in the chain. The global task, visible in full only from the top, is divided and sub-divided as the command descends towards the lower levels of the hierarchy. Once the bottom level of direct performance is reached, performers are faced with fairly straightforward and predictable choices.

Now this ideal model can work properly only on the condition that all people involved in the work of the organization follow the commands they receive and are guided only by them (their actions are, as it is said sometimes, 'rule-guided'). And that means that people should not be diverted by their personal beliefs and convictions or by emotions - sympathy or antipathy - to fellow workers or to individual clients or objects of action. Everybody's action must be totally *impersonal*; indeed, it should not be oriented to persons at all, but to the *rules*, which specify the procedure.

This kind of action directed by a codified reason of rules is described as *procedural rationality*. What counts is following the procedure to the letter. What is decried and punished more than anything else is twisting the procedure to suit individual preferences or affections. No wonder. Even the most painstakingly worked out plan of complementary actions would not count for much if personal emotions were given free rein. Indeed, those 'affections' which co-workers of an organization are asked to lock up in their closets before they clock in, stand for the choices which are erratic, rule-free, and hence impossible to predict and even less to control. Emotions, as it were, come from nowhere and unannounced; and when they come, it is virtually impossible to fight them back. One cannot commission emotions to order, neither can one send them away. Reason, calculation, memorizing the contents of the statute books, and the most painstaking design - none of these will help here.

But it is not just the wayward, 'centrifugal' sentiments that are unwelcome. To be effective, an organization does not need the affection of its members, nor their approval for the goals it genuinely or putatively serves and the task it performs. Were the members' readiness to fulfil their duty grounded in their enthusiasm for the declared purposes of their joint activity, if their performance depended on what they thought about the organization's loyalty to its ends, they would, so to speak, watch the hands of the givers of the command, and measure the orders against their ostensible purposes. In the end they might disagree with their reasons and even disobey them. Thus consent to the objectives of the organization one works for is not necessary; making it a requirement would prove downright harmful.

There are only two kinds of affection that organizations need (and thus promote) to work effectively. One is loyalty to the corporation and readiness to fulfil one's duty - independently of the contents of the work one is told to perform - providing the command was 'legitimate', that it came from the right source and through the right channels. The other is loyalty to fellow members - the 'we are all in one boat' feeling, the 'I cannot let them down' attitude. These are the only two emotions procedural rationality' needs - and in order to secure them, all other emotions must be toned down or chased out of court.

The most prominent among the exiled emotions are moral sentiments; that resilient and unruly 'voice of conscience' that may prompt one to help the sufferer and to abstain from causing suffering. Conscience may tell that the action one was told to take is wrong - even if it is procedurally correct. Or that a quite different kind of action is right, even if from the point of view of the binding procedure it is 'irregular'. And if this voice is strong and other voices which could muffle it are weak, the fate of the corporate action will now be at the mercy of the moral sentiments of the individual performers. Organizations defend themselves against such an eventuality in two ways.

The first is the phenomenon described as *floating responsibility*. Providing that the member of the organization followed the rules faithfully and did what the proper superiors told him to do, it is not he who bears responsibility for whatever effect his action may have had on its objects. Who does, then? The question is notoriously mind-boggling, as every other member of the organization also follows procedure and commands. It seems that the organization is ruled by *nobody* - that is, it is moved only by the impersonal logic of self-propelling principles. This is not, however, the only problem - as to pinpoint responsibility is even more difficult because of the minute division of labour. Each member contributing to the final effects performs, more often than not, actions which by themselves are quite innocuous, and would not - could not - cause the effects in question without the complementary actions of many other people. In a large organization most members do not even see (or hear of) the ultimate, remote and always oblique results which they help to materialize. So they may go on feeling moral and decent persons (which they mostly are when hobnobbing with their friends and family) even while helping to commit the most gruesome cruelties.

The second is the tendency to declare that most things which members of organizations are expected to do when in service are exempt from moral evaluation - they are, so to speak, ethically indifferent, neither good or bad; only correct or incorrect. This does not mean contesting commonly held moral opinions. Rather it is to declare, bluntly, that categories of 'good' and 'evil' are neither here nor there when it comes to the implementation of organizational duties. The sole standards by which such duties can be judged are those of procedural correctness; if they pass this muster, there is no other test left to which they could conceivably be put. When 'ethics' appears in the vocabulary of bureaucracy, it is in connection with 'professional ethics'; the latter is considered breached when a member shows disloyalty to the organization (by leaking secret information, using the office for purposes not foreseen by the statute books, or otherwise allowing outside interests to interfere), or disloyalty to colleagues (charges of this kind are more often than not raised on the initiative of members who believe they have been offended or harmed; the language of ethics, notoriously less exact than that of the codified rules, is reverted to whenever defined competencies are open to multiple and contentious interpretations).

All in all, modern organization is a contraption designed to make human actions immune from what the actors believe and feel privately. Here, discipline is the sole responsibility, which puts paid to all other responsibilities while the ethical code spelling out one's duties toward the organization preempts the moral questions which could be addressed to the members' behaviour. In other words, the modern organization is the way of doing things that is free from moral constraints. Because of that, cruel deeds can in principle be perpetrated by modern organizations from which individual members acting on their own would most certainly recoil in horror. Even if this does not happen, though, one harmful effect is virtually unavoidable: people who come within the orbit of bureaucratic action cease to be responsible moral subjects, are deprived of their moral autonomy and are trained not to exercise (nor trust) their moral judgment. They are cast in what the American psychologist Stanley Milgram called the 'agentic state' - in which they cease, at least for the duration, to be responsible for their actions and the consequences of their action - and plug their ears tightly so as not to hear the voice of conscience.

If *procedural* rationality is the constructive principle of organization - *instrumental* rationality is what makes business tick. Here are the ends, here are the means; here are the resources, here are the effects one can achieve if one applies them wisely. Means are to be used to the greatest possible effect; there is no greater crime in the business world than the underuse of resources, letting some assets which could 'work' and 'bring results' lie fallow and rust. How much the available means may bring is the only question one can ask about their alternative uses. Other questions - moral questions prominent among them - are given short shrift in advance; they are dismissed on the grounds that they do not make business sense, the only sense business may recognize. The virtues of ethical investments or green products tend to be recognised only when the language of morality itself 'makes good business sense', not when there are clear trade-offs to be made.

There is no denying that business, just like bureaucracy, is eager to spell out and to guard its own special kind of morality, sometimes called 'business ethics'. The paramount value of that ethics is honesty, which, as the small print shows, is mostly concerned with keeping promises and abiding by contractual obligations. Without such honesty, business cannot survive. By insisting that all sides to the contract ought to be bound by the 'honesty' principle, business partners defend themselves against the danger of being conned or short-changed.

Even more importantly though, they create for themselves a relatively orderly, predictable environment, without which instrumentally-rational decision-making would be inconceivable. And yet as with any ethical code, 'business ethics' is as much about declaring certain kinds of conduct ethically imperative, as about making other kinds of action, by commission or by omission, ethically neutral, or not moral issues at all. The code spells out how far honesty must reach and when one can say that someone was 'honest enough'. Everything stretching beyond this boundary is of no concern for business ethics; businesspeople have the right to consider themselves perfectly within their moral duty while not worrying about them.

Modern times started with the separation of business from the household. Indeed, without such a separation the instrumental logic of business would be forever contaminated, and cramped, by moral obligations. Inside the household, goods are given to people because of who they are - children, sisters, parents - and not *in order to* attain the gains the giver hopes to achieve. To make business sense, on the other hand, assets must be allocated to the highest bidder - not to those who may need them most, but those who are prepared to give most in exchange. Who the highest bidder is, the nature of their credentials and entitlements (except solvency, of course), should not matter. In business there are no friends and no neighbours. Indeed, it might even helps if the partner of a transaction is a complete stranger and remains so, since only then may instrumental rationality gain the uncontested ascendancy it needs; knowing too much of them may - who knows? - lead to a personal, emotional relationship, which will inevitably confuse and cloud judgement. Like the *esprit de corps* of corporative bureaucracy, the spirit of business militates against sentiments, the moral sentiments most prominent among them. It cannot be easily squared with the sense of responsibility for the welfare and well-being of those who may find themselves affected by the business pursuit of greatest effects. In business language, 'rationalization' means more often than not laying off people who used to derive their livelihood from serving business tasks before. They are now 'redundant', because a more effective way to use the assets has been found - and their past services do not count for much. Each business transaction, to be truly rational, must start from scratch, forgetting past merits and debts of gratitude. Business rationality shirks responsibility for its own consequences, and this is another mortal blow to the influence of moral considerations. The horrors of inner cities, mean streets, once thriving and now dying communities orphaned by business ventures which used to keep them alive, but now - for the soundest and most rational of reasons - moved to greener pastures, are not victims of exploitation, but of abandonment resulting from moral indifference.

Bureaucracy strangles or criminalises moral impulses, while business merely pushes them aside. Horrified by the totalitarian tendencies ingrained in every bureaucracy, Orwell sounded an alarm against the prospect of 'the boot eternally trampling a human face'. An apt metaphor for the business variety of morality-bashing would be perhaps 'the blinkers eternally preventing the human face from being seen'. The short-term consequences for people exposed to one or the other of the two strategies may be starkly different, yet the long-term results are quite similar: taking moral issues off the agenda, sapping the moral autonomy of the acting subject, undermining the principle of moral responsibility for the effects, however distant and indirect, of one's deeds. Neither modern organization nor modern business promotes morality; if anything, they make the life of a stubbornly moral person tough and unrewarding.

Reflecting on the perpetrators' inability not just to admit, but to comprehend their responsibility for the Holocaust crimes (these people were following orders... There was that task to be fulfilled, that job to be done... They could not let their mates down...), Hannah Arendt, a most acute interrogator of the ethical accomplishments and neglects of the modern era, demanded that 'human beings be capable of telling right from wrong even if all they have to guide them is their own judgement, which, moreover, happens to be completely at odds with what they must regard as the unanimous opinion of all around them...'

However nebulous such a demand may seem in a world dominated by bureaucracy and business, Arendt saw in it the last hope of morality, and in all probability the only realistic, however tenuous, strategy to recover for morality the ground from which it has been exiled. In the effort to meet that demand, she wrote, 'there are no rules to abide by... as there are no rules for the unprecedented'. In other words, no one else but the moral person themselves must take responsibility for their own moral responsibility.

Fragmentation and Discontinuity

The story so far has not been just about the distant past. The bureaucratic spirit of large corporations and 'business ethics' remain very much salient marks of our times and any obituaries to moral dangers they portend would be premature. They are no longer, however, the sole sources of the twin processes of 'moral neutralization' and 'flotation of responsibility' - both of which are still going strong, though taking somewhat new forms. There are quite a few new elements in the emerging human situation, which in all probability carry far-reaching moral consequences.

These new elements stem from the overall tendency to dismantle, deregulate and dissipate the once solid and relatively lasting frames in which the concerns and efforts of most individuals were inscribed. Jobs, once seen as 'for life', are more often that not now temporary and may disappear virtually without notice, together with the factories or offices or bank branches which offered them. Even the skills which the jobs required are ageing fast, turning overnight from assets into liabilities. Being prudent and provident, thinking of the future, becomes ever more difficult, as there is little sense in accumulating skills for which tomorrow there may be no demand, or saving money which tomorrow may lose much of its purchasing power. At the moment young men and women enter the game of life, none can tell what the rules of the game will be like in the future. Their only certainty is that the rules will change many times over before the game is finished.

The world, in other words, seems less solid than it used to be (or than we thought it to be). It has lost its apparent unity and continuity - when various aspects of life could be tied together into a meaningful whole, and what happened today could be traced back to its roots and forward to its consequences. What most of us learn from our experience now, is that all forms in the world around us, however solid they may seem, are not immune to change; that things burst into attention without warning and then disappear or sink into oblivion without trace; that what is all the rage today becomes the butt of ridicule tomorrow; that what is vaunted and recommended and hammered home today is treated with disdain tomorrow (if it's still remembered); that, on the whole, time is cut into episodes - each with a beginning and an end but without pre-history or future; that there is little or no logical connection between the episodes, even their succession looking suspiciously as if purely coincidental, contingent and random; and that since they come from nowhere, episodes go by and away without leaving lasting consequences. In other words, the world we live in (and help to bring about through our life pursuits) appears to be marked by *fragmentation*, *discontinuity*, and *inconsequentiality*.

In such a world, it is wise and prudent not to make long-term plans or invest into the distant future (one can never guess what the attractiveness of the present seductive goals or the value of today's assets will then be); not to get tied down too firmly to any particular place, group of people, cause, even an image of oneself, because one might find oneself not just un-anchored and drifting but without an anchor altogether; to be guided in today's choices not by the wish to *control* the future, but by the reluctance to *mortgage* it. In other words, 'to be provident' means now more often than not to avoid *commitment*. To be free to move when opportunity knocks. To be free to leave when it stops knocking.

Today's culture reiterates what each of us learns, joyfully or grudgingly, from our own experience. It presents the world as a collection of fragments and episodes, with one image chasing away and replacing the one before, only to be replaced itself moments later. Celebrities emerge and vanish daily, and only very few leave footprints. Problems commanding attention are born by the hour and slip away as soon as they are born - together with the popular concern they gave birth to. Attention has become the scarcest of resources. In the words of George Steiner, our culture has turned into a sort of 'cosmic casino', where everything is calculated 'for maximal impact and instant obsolescence'; maximal impact, since the constantly shocked imagination has become *blasé*, needing ever more powerful shocks to spur it, each one more shattering than the last; and instant obsolescence, since attention has limited capacity and room must be made to absorb new celebrities, fashions, foibles, or 'problems'.

Marshall McLuhan is remembered for coining the phrase 'the medium is the message'- meaning that whatever is the content of the message, the qualities of the media which conveyed it are themselves a message (though hidden and surreptitious), and as a rule more seminal than the content of the overt communication. One may say that if the medium which was the message of modern times was photographic paper, its equivalent for the new times is video-tape. Photographic paper can be used once only - there is no second chance. But when used, it retains the trace for a long time to come - in practical terms, forever. Think of the family album, filled with yellowing portraits of grand- and great-grandfathers and mothers, innumerable aunts and uncles, all with a name attached, all *counting and to be reckoned with*, all adding their stones to the castle of the slowly accumulating family tradition, in which no part can be taken away or eradicated, in which everything is, for better or worse, forever... And think now of the video-tape, made in such a way as to be erased, and re-used, and re-used again: to record whatever may seem interesting or amusing at the moment, but to keep it no longer than the interest lasts - after all, it is bound to wane. If the photographic paper oozed the message that deeds and things matter, tend to last and have consequences, that they tend to tie together and affect each other - the video-tape exudes the message that all things exist by themselves and count only until further notice, that each episode starts from scratch, and whatever its consequences may be erased without trace, leaving the tape virgin-clean. Or, to use a different metaphor for the difference between the two 'spirit of the time' messages, one may say that if the catchword of modern times was *creation*, the catchword of our times is *recycling*. Or again: if the favourite building material of modernity was steel and concrete, today it is rather the bio-degradable plastic.

With what consequences for morality? Quite obviously, enormous. As the greatest ethical philosopher of our century, Emmanuel Levinas, puts it morality means *being-for* (not merely being-aside or even being-with) the Other. To take a moral stance means to assume responsibility for the Other; to act on the assumption that the well-being of the Other is a precious thing calling for my effort to preserve and enhance it, that whatever I do or do not do affects it, that if I have not done it, it might not have been done at all, and that even if others do or can do it this does not cancel my responsibility for doing it myself... And this being-for is unconditional (that is, if it is *to be moral*, not merely *contractual*) - it does not depend on what the Other is, or does, whether s/he deserves my care or repays in kind. One cannot conceive of an argument that could justify the renouncing of moral responsibility - putting it in cold storage, lending or pawning. And one cannot imagine a point at which one could say with any sort of moral right: 'I have done my share, and here my responsibility ends.'

If this is what morality is about, it certainly does not square well with the discontinuous, fragmentary, episodic, consequences-avoiding life. Ours is the age of what Anthony Giddens perceptively described as 'pure relationship' which 'is entered for its own sake, for what can be derived by each person' and so 'it can be terminated, more or less at will, by either partner at any particular point'; of 'confluent love' which jars with the 'for-ever, one-and-only' qualities of the romantic love complex so that 'romance can no longer be equated with permanence', of 'plastic sexuality', that is sexual enjoyment 'severed from its age-old integration with reproduction, kinship and the generations'. We can see that to keep the options open, to be free to move is the guiding principle of all three. 'I need more space' is the curt yet common excuse used by all those who do move away - meaning 'I do not wish others to intrude, such others as I wished yesterday to intrude; I wish to be concerned solely with myself, with what is good and desirable for me'. Whoever seeks more space, must be careful not to commit themselves, and particularly not to allow commitments to outlast the pleasure which can be derived from them. They must therefore cleanse acts of possible consequences, and if consequences do follow, then - and in advance - refuse all responsibility for them.

The life of modern man was frequently likened to the pilgrimage-through-time. The itinerary of pilgrims is drawn in advance by the destination they want to reach (which in the case of modern man's life is the ideal image of a vocation, an identity) - and everything they do is calculated to bring them closer to the goal. The pilgrim is consistent in choosing every successive step, conscious that each step matters and the sequence cannot be reversed. Today's men and women can hardly treat their life as a pilgrimage, even if they wished to. One can plan one's life as a journey-to-a-destination only in a world in which one can sensibly hope that its chart will remain the same or little changed throughout the lifetime - and this is blatantly not the case today. Instead, the life of the men and women of our times is more like that of the tourists-through-time: they cannot and would not decide in advance what places they would visit and what the sequence of stations would be; what they know for sure is that they will keep on the move, never sure whether the place they reach is their final destination. Whoever knows that, is unlikely to strike deep roots anywhere and develop too strong an attachment to the locals. What they are likely to do is to treat each place as a temporary stay, significant only through the satisfactions one derives from it; but one must be ready to move again, whenever satisfaction diminishes or whenever greener pastures beckon elsewhere.

In other words, the 'I need space' strategy militates against any moral stance. It denies the moral significance of even the most intimate inter-human action. As a result, it exempts core elements of human inter-relationships from moral evaluation. It *neutralizes* the parts of human existence which the neutralizing mechanisms of bureaucracy and business could not (or did not need, or wish to) reach...

As in the case of the older forms of neutralizing moral evaluations and of the flotation of responsibility, this is not a situation that can be rectified by moral preachers (not by the preachers acting alone at any rate). Its roots lie deep in the life-context of contemporary men and women; it represents, one may say, a kind of 'rational adaptation' to the new conditions in which life is lived. These conditions favour some strategies while making other strategies terribly difficult to follow. The odds against taking a moral stance and sticking to it through thick and thin are formidable - all the socially generated pressures sap the emotional bonds between people, favouring free-floating agents. Nothing short of changing the odds will regain for morality the areas now 'emancipated from moral constraints'.

The Privatisation of Common Fates

Michael Schluter and David Lee, two shrewd observers of the moral plight of contemporary men and women, caustically commented on the way we tend to live today:

We wear privacy like a pressure suit. Given half the chance we'll stuff the seat next to ours in a cafe with raincoats and umbrellas, stare unremittingly at posters about measles in a doctor's waiting room... Anything but invite encounter; anything but get involved... (T)he home itself has grown lean and mean, wider families being broken up into nuclear and single-parent units where the individual's desires and interests characteristically take precedence over those of the group. Unable to stop treading on each other's toes in the mega-community, we have stepped into our separate houses and closed the door, and then stepped into our separate rooms and closed the door. The home becomes a multi-purpose leisure centre where household members can live, as it were, separately side by side. Not just the gas industry but life in general has been privatised.

Separately side by side. Privatised. Sharing space, but not thoughts or sentiments - and acutely aware that in all probability we no longer share fates either. This awareness does not necessarily breed resentment or hatred, but it certainly propagates aloofness and indifference. 'I do not want to get involved' is what we say more often than not to silence inchoate emotions and nip in the bud the shoots of a deeper, intimate human relationship of the 'for richer for poorer, till death us do part' kind. Ever more ingenious locks, bolts and burglar alarms are one of the few growth industries - not just for their genuine or putative practical uses, but for their symbolic value. Inwardly, they mark the boundary of the hermitage where we won't be disturbed, while outwardly they communicate our decision: 'for all I care, outside could be a wasteland'.

We have explored some of the causes of this deepening aloofness and indifference. Not all, though. The 'privatisation of life in general' has long tentacles and reaches far and wide. Privatised life, like any other life, is never an unremitting bliss. It has its measure of suffering, discontent and grievance. In a privatised life, however, misfortune is as private as everything else. The misfortunes of privatised singles do not add up, each one pointing as it seems in a different direction and each calling for different remedies. In the privatised society of ours, grievances seem to point in widely divergent directions and even clash with each other; they seldom cumulate and condense into a common cause. In a shifting, drifting world, what possible benefit may an individual derive from joining forces with another piece of flotsam?

The distinguished German-English sociologist Norbert Elias pondered on the lessons one might draw from Edgar Allan Poe's famous story of the three seamen caught in the maelstrom. In the story, two of the seamen died - not so much sucked in by the raging sea, as pushed down by their own paralysis born of despair and fear - while the third, having cast an alert eye around and noticed that round objects tend to float rather than being drawn into the whirl, promptly jumped into a barrel and survived. Well, since the times of Diogenes, barrels have been notorious symbols of the ultimate withdrawal from the world, the ultimate individual retreat. Norbert Elias intended his commentary as a consolation: look, even in the midst of storm reason will point the way out... But note that the message reason whispers in this particular storm is: each one of you, look for a barrel to hide in.

Recent years have been marked by a slow yet relentless dismantling or weakening of agencies which used to institutionalize the *commonality* of fate, and their replacement with institutions expressing and promoting the *diversity* of fate. The intended or unintended effect of the process is to re-cast the community (and communal action in general) from being the source of individual security into the individual's burden and bane; an extra load to carry, adding little to the individual's personal well-being, yet something one cannot, regrettably, easily shake off though one would dearly like to. Increasingly, we confront the community's common needs and causes solely in the capacity of taxpayers; it is no more the question of our shared responsibility for, and collective insurance against, everyone's mishap and misfortune - but the question of how much it will cost me to provide for those who cannot provide for themselves. *Their* claims testify to the fact that they are *spongers*, though *my* demands to pay less into the kitty most emphatically do not. It is only natural that the taxpayer wants to pay fewer taxes (just as the beast of burden wants the burden to be smaller). The outcome is, of course, that the quality of services collectively provided slides down a steep slope. And then everyone who can afford the price of a barrel buys one and jumps into it. When possible, we buy ourselves individually out of the under-provided shabby schools, overcrowded, undernourished hospitals or miserly old-age pensions - as we have already bought ourselves, with the consequences which most of us belatedly bewail, out of shrinking and wilting public transport systems. The more we do so, the more reasons we have for doing it, as the schools grow shabbier, hospital queues longer, and old-age provisions more miserly still; and the fewer reasons we see to make sacrifices for the sake of those who failed to follow suit. Were Marie Antoinette miraculously transported into the present, she would probably say: 'they complain that the common boat has got rusty and unseaworthy? Why do they not buy barrels?'

There is a point somewhere down the slope, now perhaps passed, at which people find it very hard to conceive of any benefit they could derive from joining forces: of any improvement which could come from managing a part of their resources jointly, rather than individually. (For many years now the burden of taxation, though showing no signs of lessening, has been shifted steadily from taxing income to taxing consumption. The trend is widely applauded and welcomed. Many people seem to enjoy the brief interlude of freedom between cashing a cheque and signing another one). The weaker and less reliable are the guarantees of individual security communally offered, the less justified and more burdensome seem the communal claims for joint effort and sacrifice. It is now more often than not a 'your value for my money' situation. And as the numbers of those who give money overtake the numbers of those deprived of value, the fate of the spongers is sealed. Their claims and grievances have every chance of being voted off the agenda democratically, by the majority of the beneficiaries of our universal right to vote.

But neglect of the less fortunate is not the only result. It can only come, as it does, together with the general fading and demise of the community spirit. If politics (things that are discussed and decided in the *agora*, where all those interested may congregate and speak) is about things of *common* interest and significance, who needs politics when interests and meanings keep steering apart? Interest in politics always had its ups and downs, but now we seem to be witnessing a totally new incarnation of electoral apathy. Today's disenchantment seems to reach deeper than the traditional frustration with unkept promises or programmes without vision. It hits politics as such. It shows that the majority of the electors can no longer see why they should be bothered because so little seems to depend on what 'they' say or even do out there.

The 'citizens' charters', one of the few recent attempts to find a new connection between citizens and their shared services, confirm the trend. Their remarkable characteristic is that they construe citizens not as people eager to assume responsibility for issues larger than their private needs and desires, but as consumers of services provided by agencies they have little right and no interest to examine, let alone supervise. Citizens' charters promote that image of the citizen by defining citizen rights as first and foremost, perhaps even solely, the right of the customer to be satisfied. This includes the right to complain and to compensation. This does not include, conspicuously, the right to look into the inner workings of the agencies complained about and expected to pay the compensation - much less the right to tell them what to do.

There is a sort of a vicious circle. An increasingly privatised life feeds disinterest in politics. And politics, freed from constraints, deepens the extent of privatisation, thus breeding more indifference. Or perhaps this is a case of a gordian knot so twisted that one can no more say where the string of determinations starts and where it leads to. The chances, therefore, that moral responsibilities eroded at the grassroots level will be resuscitated by a moral vision promoted by the eroded institutions of the common wealth, are slim. The odds against are enormous.

Few if any grievances or hopes are nowadays addressed to the government of the country - not with much realistic expectation that they will be acted on, anyway. Even grievances and hopes have generally been redefined as private concerns. In this country, the tendency has been exacerbated by the far-reaching weakening of many of the 'middle-range' institutions particularly in local government. So much power has been taken away from the town halls, so little depends on what they do, so toothless have trade unions become, that a reasonable person seeking redress or improvement would rather look elsewhere. All in all, the new spirit is sceptical about the possible uses and benefits of acting together and joining forces, and is resigned to the idea that whatever you want to achieve, you had better look to your own cunning and ingenuity as the principal resources. Lady Thatcher might have committed a grave factual error when she said that there is no such thing as 'society'; but she certainly allowed no mistake as to the objectives her legislative efforts pursued. What the ill-famed proposition reported were the speaker's intentions, and the subsequent years went far towards making the word flesh.

But do we not act in solidarity - at least on occasion? Time and again we hear of people gathering to promote or defend a cause they seem to consider to be shared by them all. Without that 'sharing of feelings', there would be no public meetings, marches or collecting of signatures. True enough. And yet more often than not common actions do not live long enough to create new institutions that can command the stable loyalty of their participants. Like other events, they briefly burst into attention and fade away to give room for other preoccupations. They are on the whole 'single issue' actions, gathering around one demand people of varied persuasions, who often make very strange bedfellows and who have little else in common. Only rarely do such single issues manifest or enhance the sentiment of moral responsibility for common welfare. Much more often they mobilize sentiments *against*, not *for*: against a bypass or a rail link, against a Romany camp or travellers' convoy, against a dumping ground for toxic waste. Sometimes it seems that their main goal is not to make the shared world better and more habitable, but rather to redistribute its less prepossessing aspects: dumping the awkward and unpleasant parts of it in the neighbours' backyard. They divide more than they unite. Obliquely, they promote the idea that different people have different moral entitlements, and that the rights of some entail the right to deny rights of some others.

A privatised existence has its many joys: freedom of choice, the opportunity to try many ways of life, the chance to make oneself to the measure of one's self-image. But it has its sorrows as well - loneliness and incurable uncertainty as to the choices made and still to be made being foremost among them. It is not an easy matter to build one's own identity relying on one's own guesses and hunches alone. And there is little reassurance to be drawn from the self-made identity if it has not been recognized and confirmed by a power stronger and longer-lasting than the solitary builder. Identity must be seen as such; the dividing line between a socially accepted and an individually imagined identity is one between self-assertion and madness. This is why we all feel time and again an overwhelming 'need of belonging' - a need to identify ourselves not just as individual human beings, but as members of a larger entity. That identification-through-membership is hoped to provide a firm foundation on which to erect a smaller and feebler personal identity. As some of the old, once solid, entities underwriting and endorsing individual identities lie in ruins, while others are fast losing their holding power, there is a demand for new ones, able to pronounce authoritative and binding judgments.

The Deficiencies of Community

We are being told repeatedly by many on both left and right that the *community* is the most likely candidate to fill the gap. Yet modernity spent most of its time and a lot of its energy on fighting communities - those larger than life groupings into which people are born, only to be held inside them for the rest of their lives by the dead hand of tradition strengthened by collective surveillance and blackmail. From the Enlightenment on, it has been seen as a commonsensical truth that human emancipation, the releasing of genuine human potential, required that the bounds of communities should be broken and individuals set free from the circumstances of their birth. We seem to have come full circle now. The idea of community has been recovered from the cold storage where modernity bent on boundless humanity confined it, and restored to a genuine or imaginary past glory. It is on the community that many hopes bereaved by bankrupt or discredited institutions now focus. What had been once rejected as a constraint is now hailed as the 'enabling capacity'. What was once seen as an obstacle on the road to full humanity, is now praised as its necessary condition. Humanity, we are told, comes in many forms and shapes, and thanks to communities, traditions and cultures, the inherited forms of life are here to see to it that this is the case.

Social thought was always keen to repeat the stories told or merely thought of by the power-holders, and to disguise their intentions and ambitions as descriptions of social reality, of its laws or its 'historical tendencies'. During the age of the modern cultural crusades launched against regional, local or ethnic self-management, self-congratulating obituaries of communities filled social-scientific treatises. But powers eager to present their own particularity as human universality are today thin in the field, and there is naturally not much point in narrating their by now faded dreams. The new powers that took their place do not speak the language of universality. On the contrary, they appeal to what *distinguishes* one human collectively from another. To gain more grip on their own territories and without hope or urge to encroach on the territories of the others, they are ready to admit that the plurality of human forms is here to stay: no more a regrettable yet temporary flaw, but a permanent feature of human existence. And social thought, promptly and obligingly, changes the tune.

The argument about the supremacy of supposedly 'natural' community in the life of the individual runs as follows: each one of us is born into a certain tradition and language, which decides what to see before we begin to look, what to say before we learn to speak, what to consider important before we start weighing things against each other, and how to conduct ourselves before we start pondering the choices. Thus in order to know what we are, to understand ourselves, we must fathom and consciously embrace that tradition; and in order to be ourselves, to keep our identity intact and waterproof, we must support that tradition with all our heart. In fact, we owe it our complete loyalty; and we ought to offer its demands an unquestionable priority whenever loyalty calls in that society of multiple loyalties clash.

The argument, as it were, reverses the true order of things. Traditions do not 'exist' by themselves and independently of what we think and do; they are daily re-invented by our dedication, our selective memory and selective seeing, our way of behaving *as if* they defined our conduct. The communities are *postulated*; and the meaning of their being 'real' is that many people, in unison, follow that postulate. The call to give the 'community of belonging' our prime and undivided loyalty, the demand to consider ourselves the community member first, and all the rest later, is precisely the way to make community a 'reality', to split the larger society into little enclaves which eye each other with suspicion and keep at a distance from each other. And because these communities, unlike modern nations well entrenched in the coercive and educational institutions of the nation-state, do not have many legs to stand on except our individual loyalties, they require an unusually intense emotional dedication and shrill, vociferous and spectacular declarations of faith; and they sniff in the half-hearted, lukewarm and undecided fringes the most mortal of dangers.

So there is another contradiction between the 'community narrative' and the true state of affairs it narrates. The siren-song of community is all about the warmth of togetherness, mutual understanding and love; such a relief from the cold, harsh and lonely life of competition and continuous uncertainty. Community advertises itself as the cosy home amidst a hostile and dangerous city; it draws profusely, overtly or obliquely, on the very contemporary image of the sharp divide between the fortified and electronically protected homestead and the street full of knife-carrying strangers, the wasteland subjected to a chary 'neighbourhood watch'. Community seduces its proselytes with the promise of freedom from fear and the tranquillity of *chez soi*. But again, the reality is all too often the opposite. Given the endemic brittleness of foundations, community can ill afford anything but full and militant dedication to the cause; its self-appointed guardians are day and night on the look-out, searching for real or putative traitors, turncoats or just the half-hearted and irresolute. Independence is frowned upon, dissent hounded down, disloyalty persecuted. Pressure to keep the intended flock in the fold is unrelenting; the craved-for cosiness of belonging is offered at the price of unfreedom.

The overall effect of all this is yet another case of the by now familiar tendency to expropriate the individual's moral responsibility. It is now the community, or rather the self-proclaimed wardens of its purity, who draw the boundaries of moral obligations, divide good from evil, and for better or worse dictate the definition of moral conduct. The paramount concern of their moral legislation is to keep the division between 'us' and 'them' watertight; not so much to promote moral standards, as to install *double* standards (as the French say, *deux poids, deux mésures*) - one for 'us', another reserved for the treatment of 'them'. True, unlike the depersonalised world of privatised individuals, the postulation of community neither promotes moral indifference nor suffers it lightly. But it does not cultivate moral selves either. It replaces the torments of moral responsibility with the certainty of discipline and submission. And the disciplined selves are in no way guaranteed to be moral. While the submissive selves can be easily deployed - and are deployed - in the service of the cruel, mindless inhumanity of the endless (and hopeless) inter-communal wars of attrition and boundary skirmishes.

Risk and Limits

We have come a long way in our search for the sources of moral hope, but remain, so far, empty-handed. Our only gain is that we have learnt where such sources are unlikely to be found. Bureaucracy and business were never famous as shrines of ethics and schools of morality. But nor can much be expected from the entities meant to compensate for the harm they have done to the moral backbone of human selves. Back to the family? Processes of privatisation reach deep into the heart of family life. And even making parents unpaid policemen, as those who propose fining parents for their children's misbehaviour want, would hardly stem the tide. Back into the community fold? Here, moral responsibilities are more likely to be put into deep freeze than resuscitated. More than two centuries after the Enlightenment promise to legislate for an ethical and humane society, we are left, each of us, with our own individual conscience and sentiment of responsibility as the only resource with which to struggle to make life more moral than it is. And yet we find this resource depleted and squeezed.

This is not just the matter of concern for moral philosophers and preachers. However worried they may be, there is every reason for their worry to be widely shared. The dilemma we confront now has been expressed poignantly by the great

German/American ethical philosopher, Hans Jonas: 'The very same movement which put us in possession of the powers that have now to be regulated by norms... has by a necessary complementarity eroded the foundations from which norms could be derived... Now we shiver in the nakedness of nihilism in which near-omnipotence is paired with near-emptiness, greatest capacity with knowing least what for'.

Indeed, the stakes are enormous. One of the most influential books published in the last decade was Ulrich Beck's *Risk Society*. Beck's message is that our society is becoming increasingly a risk-producing, risk-monitoring and risk-managing society. We do not so much move 'forward', as clear the mess and seek exit from the havoc perpetrated by the things we did yesterday. The risks are our own products, though unexpected and often impossible to predict or calculate. This is because whatever we do, we concentrate on the task at hand (this ability of close-focusing is in fact the secret of the astonishing achievements of science and technology), while the changes we introduce in the balance of nature and society in order to perform that task reverberate far and wide; their distant effects hit back as new dangers, new problems, and thus new tasks. What makes this already depressing plight near catastrophic, though, is that the scale of the changes we inadvertently provoke is so massive, that the line beyond which the risks become totally unmanageable and damages irreparable may be crossed at any moment. We are beginning now to attempt to calculate the dangers of climatic change caused by pollution, or of the depletion of soil and water supplies caused by ever more specialised fertilisers and insecticides. But we cannot easily count the dangers involved in releasing into nature artificially created viruses (each one, to be sure, with its specific, invariably praise-worthy, uses) or ever more rarified genetical engineering of the human species, aimed ultimately at introducing bespoke-tailor shops for human offspring? Besides, although very often we know the risks only too well, there is little we can do with our knowledge since the forces that push us deeper and deeper into increasingly risky territory are overwhelming. Think for instance of the relentless saturation of the conflict-ridden world with ever more refined and ever less resistible weapons, or of adding each year hundreds of thousands of new vehicles to the blight of congested roads and virtually stand-still traffic we all, at the moments of reflection, bemoan. Experience suggests that there is little ground to console ourselves that the same skills that make us powerful enough to produce awesome risks can also make us wise enough to reflect upon them and *therefore* do something to limit the damage. Ability to reflect does not translate easily into the ability to act.

Even if the mind is perceptive and judicious enough, the will may prove to be wanting; and even if the will is there, hands may be too short. We introduce our improvements (or medicines to heal the wounds left by earlier failed improvements) locally; yet their effects may reach the nooks and crannies of the globe so that we are only dimly aware of their presence. We act here and now, to deal with nuisances we feel today - and we act without giving ourselves enough time to think about, let alone test, the long-term effects of our doings. But will we still be able to cross that other bridge when we come to it? And what sort of a bridge will it be? Think of the new wonder drugs which one after another burst into our dreams of happiness thanks to the ingenuity of scholars and promoters. Their so called 'side-effects' are tested - sometimes over much too short, sometimes over a prudently longer period. The contraceptive pill has been taken by millions of women for over twenty years now, so we may say that we know the risks that come to the surface during this time-span. But do we really know what the human world will be like in, say, a hundred years from now, after several generations of women on the pill? And is there a way of knowing it? Or do we know the several-generations-long effects of artificial insemination and in-vitro conception?

These are serious questions, the kind of which we never had a need to ask before. We seem to require now an entirely new brand of ethics. An ethics made to the measure of the enormous distances of space and time on which we can act and on which we act even when we neither know nor intend it. The 'first duty' of such ethics, to quote Jonas again, is 'visualising the long-range effects of technological enterprise'. Such an ethics must be guided, says Jonas, by a 'heuristics of fear' and 'principle of uncertainty': even if the arguments of the pessimists and the optimists are finely balanced, 'the prophecy of doom is to be given greater heed than the prophecy of bliss'. Jonas sums up with an updated (though - as he is quick to admit himself - far from logically self-evident) version of Kant's categorical imperative: 'act so that the effects of your action are compatible with the permanence of genuine human life'. If in doubt - Jonas implies - do not do it. Do not magnify or multiply the risk more than unavoidable; err, if at all, on the side of caution.

The ethical self-limitation Jonas thinks we need is a tall order. Following the 'heuristics of fear' would mean nothing less than resisting, withstanding and defying the pressures exerted by virtually all other aspects of contemporary living: market competition, the on-going undeclared war of redistribution between territorial and non-territorial units and groups, the self-propelling and self-enhancing tendencies of technology and science, our understanding of life-process and collective living as a succession of 'problems' to be 'resolved' and our deeply ingrained dependence on ever more expert and technique-intensive solutions to problems. Behind all those other aspects stand powerful, well-entrenched institutions which lend their impact the almost elemental power of 'natural forces'. Behind the new ethical imperative, on the other hand, stands the diffuse feeling that we cannot go on like this for much longer without courting dangers of formidable, perhaps unprecedented, proportions. This feeling has not yet found its institutional haven and it is far from clear where there are the forces likely to inscribe Jonas-type principles on their banners - let alone forces powerful enough to make them victorious.

New Ethics in Search of New Politics

Hannah Arendt, a most insightful observer and severe judge of our present human condition, wrote profusely and convincingly of the 'emptiness of political space'. What she meant was that in our times there are no more obvious sites in the *body politic* of effacing past scandals and inanities from memory. Commitments are all until further notice, and eternal rights are as mortal as eternity itself has become.

A government that practices and promotes politics so understood, likes its subjects as they come, with their shifting eyes and vagrant attention, however much it waxes lyrical from time to time about a glorious heritage and old family values. Subjects who live their life as a collection of inconsequential and forgettable episodes would do nicely, thank you, for governments whose policies are a series of inconsequential (better to be forgotten) fragments. Such governments act so that nothing can be perceived as lasting and trustworthy, predictable, counted on and relied upon. They remove the places where decisions are taken to where those affected by them cannot see them as decisions, but only as 'blind fate'. They offer the play of market forces as the only pattern for life, for life lived as play, and promote 'playing your hand well' as the supreme standard of decency.

Such lives are not an unmixed bliss. Far from it. The belief in bliss endemic to a life of consumption is anything but 'trivially true'. What about uncertainty, insecurity, loneliness and the future being a site of fear instead of hope? What of never accumulating anything securely, of being sure of nothing, of being never able to say with confidence 'I have arrived'? What about seeing in the neighbourhood only a jungle to be warily and fearfully watched, in the stranger only a beast to hide from; what about the privatised prisons of burglar-proof homes?

Life has not got to be like this. The space we co-habit may be well and consensually structured; in such a space, in which many things vital to the life of each of us (transport, schools, surgeries, media of communication) are shared, we may see each other as conditions, rather than obstacles, to our well-being. Much as the fragmented and discontinuous life promotes the waning of moral impulses, a shared life of continuous and multi-faceted relationships would reinvigorate moral responsibilities and awaken the urge to shoulder the task of managing (now truly common) affairs. Much as the life of episodes and the politics reduced to crisis-management both prompt the exit from politics, sharing of responsibilities would go a long way towards helping citizens to recover the voice they lost or stopped trying to make audible.

Contemporary society speaks in many voices and we know now that it will do so for a very long time to come. The central issue of our times is how to reforge that polyphony into harmony and prevent it from degenerating into cacophony. Harmony is not uniformity; it is always an inter-play of a number of different motifs, each retaining its separate identity and sustaining the resulting melody through, and thanks to, that identity.

Hannah Arendt thought the capacity of inter-play to be the quality of the *polis* - where we can meet each other as *equals*, while recognizing our diversity, and caring for the preservation of that diversity as the very purpose of our meeting... How may this be achieved? Through the separate identities stopping short of *exclusivity*, of refusal to cohabit with other identities. This in turn requires abandoning the tendency to suppress other identities in the name of the self-assertion of one's own, while accepting, on the contrary, that it is precisely the guarding of other identities that maintains the diversity in which one's own uniqueness can thrive.

In his highly influential *Theory of Justice*, John Rawls presented the model of 'overlapping consensus', spelling out the assumptions under which the harmony between diversity and unity may be attained. This is how Richard J Mouw and Sander Griffioen summarise his propositions:

The core contention here is that while people come into the public domain from very different metaphysical/religious/moral starting points, once they have arrived they can agree to operate with the same intuitive ideas about what goes into a just arrangement. They can reach a consensus on such matters as the rule of law, liberty of conscience, freedom of thought, equality of opportunity, a fair share of material means for all citizens...

'They can'... The question is, would they? And will they? The citizens who used to meet at the public spaces of the *polis* may have managed on the whole to do it quite well. But they met there with the overt intention of discussing public matters, for which they, and they alone, bore responsibility: nowhere else will the things be done if we do not do them... Whatever overlapping consensus' there was, it was their common achievement, not the gift they received. They made and made again that consensus as they met and talked and argued. In Jeffrey Weeks' apt phrase, 'humanity is not an essence to be realised, but a pragmatic construction, a perspective, to be developed through the articulation of the variety of individual projects, of differences, which constitute our humanity in the broadest sense'.

It was the American political scientist Albert Hirschman who first suggested that people may influence the affairs which concern them in two ways: through *voice* or through *exit* (not by accident did Hirschman take as his model the actions undertaken by people in their capacity of *consumers*): 'voice' stands for demanding changes in the kind of things done and the way they are done; 'exit' - for turning one's back on disliked things altogether and going elsewhere to seek satisfaction. The difference between 'voice' and 'exit' is, to put it bluntly, one between engagement and disengagement; responsibility and indifference. We may say that if the present condition we are in needs people to make their voices audible, it is the exit that our political institutions, and the idea of 'citizen' they promote, favour.

Indeed, this is what the conception of the citizen as a satisfied customer is all about. Leave decisions to the ones in the know, and they will take care of your well-being. As to yourself, take care of things close your home: preserve *family* values. And yet we have seen that it is precisely the withdrawal into the walls of one's family (followed soon by a further withdrawal into the individual shell), losing from sight those intricate yet intimate connections between life in the family (or indeed the individual life) and life in public spaces, forgetting how much the latter determines the first - that constitutes the most grievous bodily harm which the present privatisation of human concerns delivered to the chances of moral revial. Under closer scrutiny, the alleged medicine looks suspiciously like the disease.

It is all too easy to expose other people's hopes as not firmly enough founded, and their solutions as not realistic enough. It is much more difficult to propose one's own warrants for hope and one's own solutions that would be immune to similar charges. This is not because of the shortage of imagination or good will, but because the present human condition itself is shot through with ambivalence, and any diagnosis seems to point to two opposite directions simultaneously, towards developments whose compatibility is far from evident. To put it in a nutshell: the chance of counteracting the present pressures towards draining intimate and public life of ethical motives and moral evaluations depends at the same time on more autonomy for *individual* moral selves and more vigorous sharing of *collective* responsibilities. In terms of the orthodox 'state vs. individual' dilemma, this is clearly a contradiction and promoting it seems like an effort to square the circle. And yet if any conclusions at all follow from our discussion so far, it is that the contradiction is illusory, and that the widespread uncritical acceptance of the illusion is itself a product of the tendencies which need to be rectified and of the orthodox thought that mimicked them.

We have seen that all the designed and tried artificial substitutes for spontaneous moral impulses and the individual responsibility for the Other have failed, or worse, ended up disarming the ethical safeguards against the danger of the human thrust towards control and mastery to degenerate into inhuman cruelty and oppression. We can repeat now with yet greater conviction Max Frisch's words with which we opened this discussion: at the end of our long modern march towards a reason-guided society, we are returned, as far as the terms of our coexistence are concerned, to our old resources of moral sense and fellow-feeling, guiding us in daily moral choices.

For such a guidance, we have no indubitable and universally agreed codes and rules. Choices are indeed choices, and that means that each is to some extent arbitrary and that uncertainty as to its propriety is likely to linger long after the choice was made. We understand now that uncertainty is not a temporary nuisance, which can be chased away through learning the rules, or surrendering to expert advice, or just doing what others do. Instead it is a permanent condition of life. We may say more - it is the very soil in which the moral self takes root and grows. Moral life is a life of continuous uncertainty, and it takes a lot of strength and resilience and an ability to withstand pressures to be a moral person. Moral responsibility is *unconditional* and in principle *infinite* - and thus one can recognize a moral person by their never quenched dissatisfaction with their moral performance; the gnawing suspicion that they were not moral enough.

On the other hand, a society that engages its members, as the *polis* did, in the different yet imperative task of caring for, and running common affairs so that the common life could observe the standards of justice and prudence - such a society requires neither disciplined subjects nor satisfaction-seeking consumers of socially provided services, but rather tenacious and sometimes obstinate, but always responsible, citizens. To be responsible does not mean to follow the rules; it may often require us to disregard the rules or to act in a way the rules do not warrant. Only such responsibility makes the citizen into that basis on which can be built a human community resourceful and thoughtful enough to cope with the present challenges.

Conceivably... And no more than that, since no guarantee is given that such a community will indeed be built, and since there are no foolproof methods to make sure that it is. In fact the only assurance is the relentless effort of the builders itself. What may help in this effort is the awareness of the intimate connection (not contradiction!) between autonomous, morally self-sustained and self-governed (often therefore unwieldy and awkward) citizens and a fully-fledged, self-reflective and self-correcting political community. They can only come together; neither is thinkable without the other.

Further Reading

Hannah Arendt, *The Human Condition*, Chicago 1958

Zygmunt Bauman, *Postmodern Ethics*, Oxford 1993

David Campbell & Michael Dillon, *The Political Subject of Violence*, Manchester 1993

Anthony Giddens, *The Transformation of Intimacy: Sexuality, Love and Eroticism in Modern Societies*, Cambridge 1992

Richard J. Mouw & Sander Griffioen, *Pluralism and Horizons: An Essay in Christian Public Philosophy*, Grand Rapids 1993

Geoff Mulgan, *Politics in an Antipolitical Age*, Cambridge 1994

Michael Schluter and David Lee, *The R Factor*, London 1993

Judith Squires (ed.), *Principled Positions: Postmodernism and the Rediscovery of Value*, London 1993

Arne Johan Vetlesen, *Perception, Empathy and Judgment: An Inquiry into the Preconditions of Moral Performance*, Pennsylvania 1994

Peter Wagner, *A Sociology of Modernity: Liberty and Discipline*, London 1994

Tony Wright, *Citizens and Subjects; An Essay on British Politics,* London 1994

Other Demos publications available for £5.95 post free from Demos, 9 Bridewell Place, London EC4V 6AP.

Reconnecting Taxation by Geoff Mulgan and Robin Murray. Geoff Mulgan is Director of Demos. Robin Murray works for the Government of Ontario.
ISBN 1 898309 00 0

An End to Illusions by Alan Duncan. Alan Duncan is Conservative MP for Rutland and Melton. He entered the House of Commons in 1992.
ISBN 1 898309 05 1

Transforming the Dinosaurs by Sir Douglas Hague. Sir Douglas Hague is an Associate Fellow of Templeton College, Oxford, non-executive director of CRT Group plc and President of Corporate Positioning Services.
ISBN 1 898309 10 8

The Parenting Deficit by Amitai Etzioni. Amitai Etzioni is Professor of Sociology at George Washington University. He has previously worked at Harvard Business School, the Brookings Institution and the White House.
ISBN 1 898309 20 5

Sharper Vision by Ian Hargreaves. Ian Hargreaves is Deputy Editor of the Financial Times. He was formerly Head of News and Current Affairs at the BBC.
ISBN 1 898309 25 6

The World's New Fissures by Vincent Cable. Vincent Cable is Director of the International Economics Programme at the Royal Institute for International Affairs.
ISBN 1 898309 353

The Audit Explosion by Michael Power. Michael Power is lecturer in Accounting and Finance and Coopers & Lybrand Fellow at the London School of Economics and Political Science.
ISBN 1 898 309 302

The Demos Quarterly - available for £2.50 or £3 per copy post-paid.

Issue 1 featured Howard Gardner on 'Opening Minds' and a series of articles on education. Other contributors included John Stewart and Amitai Etzioni.

Issue 2 is titled 'The End of Unemployment: bringing work to life'. Contributors included Rosabeth Moss Kanter, Paul Ormerod, Martin Wolf and Douglas Hague.

Demos

Demos is a registered charity. It is financed by voluntary donations from individuals, foundations and companies. The views expressed in publications are those of the authors alone. They do not represent Demos' institutional viewpoint.

If you wish to support Demos' activities, you can become a subscriber.

Further details available from Demos' offices; 9 Bridewell Place, London EC4V 6AP. Telephone 071 353 4479 Fax 071 353 4481.